Green and Profitable

BOOK 2

Marketing Strategy/Messages For Green Businesses

Shel Horowitz

Green and Profitable Book 2: Marketing Strategy/Messages for
Green Business
©2015, Shel Horowitz

ISBN-13: 978-1511418805
ISBN-10: 151141880X

Printed in the United States of America
10, 9, 8, 7, 6, 5, 4, 3, 2

Published by AWM Books - Hadley, MA

Contents

Raising the Bar on Green Marketing

The old green messages are beginning to look a bit pale. Accusations of greenwashing are rife, and often, those charges have more than a little substance—does anyone really believe BP is a green company anymore?

So does that mean green marketing is dead? What's a conscious marketer to do?

First of all, I don't for a moment believe that green is dying, let alone dead. But just as parents stop diapering their babies once they've been toilet trained and expect them to wipe their own tushes from that point on, so we as green marketers need to take greater responsibility for our messaging. Like those toddlers who are mastering not only toilet training but walking and talking and table manners and a whole bunch of other stuff all at once, we have to stand on our own feet, even if it feels a bit wobbly at first.

So here are a few marketing guideposts on your own wobble toward sustainable marketing:

1) Be clear and specific. Today's informed consumer doesn't just want to hear "we've gone green." They'll respond better to something like "by introducing this new, efficient packing machine,

we've reduced solid waste by 18 percent and cut carbon emissions by 368 tons a year."

2) Make consumers understand what each of these accomplishments means to them: "That solid waste reduction means we don't have to bring nearly as much to the landfill, which means lower costs passed on to you, longer landfill life, and fewer non-degradable materials clogging up the landfill. Lower carbon means 68 fewer asthma cases in our county every year, as well as reducing catastrophic global warming."

3) If you're familiar with the concept of features vs. benefits, you'll note that the first bullet stresses features—which are by themselves seldom enough to sell successfully—and the second bullet translates those features into direct benefits both to the consumer and to the world. Features let the gear-heads (who already understand what they mean) supply the benefits themselves); benefits speak to average consumers through their own emotional needs and wants, and are much more powerful. In many cases, you need both.

4) Raise the bar on your industry's standards for going green. Have you achieved zero waste in a facet of production? Have you not just switched to compostable plastics but actually begun to compost them? Have you figured out a way to cut energy or water use by some huge percentage? Are you sourcing a larger percentage of materials from sustainable-practices vendors? Say so! You'll get the competitive advantage of doing this before

others—and once your competitors start imitating, you can still get good marketing mileage out of having been first.

Stay away from messaging that won't be believed. If you're promoting nuclear power or large-scale biomass, for example, any attempt to portray your company as green will come back to bite you. Best, of course, is not to promote those products at all, but if you have to promote them, get out of the green space and find other ways to market (or should I say, defend) these environmentally toxic technologies. Both of these have been promoted as green alternatives, and neither one passes the sniff test.

If the green content of your practices is questionable or largely unknown, be prepared to document it in your messaging—thoroughly.

I went to a solar festival where a couple of the exhibitors were talking about "biochar." From their materials, it looked to me like just another variant on burning wood: points for renewability, certainly, but NOT for clean emissions or carbon impact reduction.

By failing to convince me that they were truly green, these companies left me highly skeptical of other claims they (or their competitors) might make.

As I learned more about biochar over the next few years, I became convinced that there actually is merit in the green argument for biochar. But these first vendors I encountered didn't make a strong enough case.

Involve your supply chain. Just as "no man is an island," neither is a corporation. You have vendors who sell to you, and customers who buy from you. You have ancillary services involved, such as transportation or security. And you have both carrot- and stick-flavored leverage you can exert to help these companies go green. The carrots: not only will they get more of your business, but you will promote them in your green marketing campaigns. The stick? If they fail your sustainability criteria, you'll choose another vendor who is more earth-centered.

consumers that there are sustainable alternatives, pressures competitors to also go green, and continues to generate momentum toward a better world.

Don't Hide Your Light!

The box says "100% of the electricity used to manufacture these crackers and this container come from green power sources," and has a nice little accompanying graphic of a windmill. Just above this is a Forest Stewardship Council certification logo denoting sustainably harvested timber sources for the box.

This is a company that's doing the right thing, right?

Wrong. Both of these logos and statements are on the bottom panel of the box, where no one can see it unless they've already bought the crackers—or perhaps if the prospect accidentally knocks the package off the supermarket shelf, happens to land the bottom facing up, and somehow notices the small logos while picking up the box.

In other words, the marketing benefit of their commitment is just slightly above zero.

This particular package has plenty of white space on the front panel, prime real estate that does have a heksher (Kosher certification logo) but otherwise, does very little marketing at all.

This cracker company (which I will not name publicly) is far from alone.

Another example, which I highlight as a case study in my talks, is the household paper products company, Marcal. When I ask my audiences what year they think Marcal switched to recycled paper, most of the answers tend to fall between 1985 and 2005. Occasionally someone will guess a year in the 1970s, especially if I call the company a pioneer in using recycled stock.

Not once has anyone guessed the correct answer—1950—or even the correct decade. Because, for too long, like the cracker company, Marcal kept its best marketing point hidden. Even though the company has been 100% recycled for more than 60 years, it was only in the  past decade that it started incorporating this vital message into its packaging—and only since 2009 that environmental branding has become the central focus of its message to consumers.

You just have to wonder how much more toilet paper, napkins, tissues and paper towels the company would have sold if it had started bragging earlier. I know that when I first became aware of environmental concerns in the early 1970s, I would have been thrilled to find a cost-competitive brand that was also very green.

Like Marcal, the Swiss cereal company Familia has been using sustainable practices—in this case, buying grains from sustainable farms—for decades. But it was only early in 2010 that I noticed this was finally explained on its packaging.

These are three examples among hundreds.

Why do companies take the time and trouble to do good in th
world, and then act like they're embarrassed about it? Perhaps it's
matter of corporate humility, not wanting to brag. In some case
maybe it's worry about being accused of greenwashing—a
accusation that could definitely hurt.

In Marcal's case, it may have started as a legitimate fear that peopl
wouldn't buy household paper made of other people's castoffs, eve
if it was just their sterilized junkmail. In the conformist, status
conscious 1950s, it may not have been seen as a marketing strengtl
but as a liability.

But certainly by 1980 if not well before, what we now call Cultura
Creatives were a well-established and rapidly growing marketin
demographic. As far back as the 2000 publication of their book, _Th_
Cultural Creatives: How 50 Million People Are Changing the World
Paul H. Ray and Sherry Ruth Anderson estimated that more than
quarter of all adults in the developed countries they studied fell intc
this category. A quarter of the population!

Greenwashing accusations are easily defused
with one simple rule: tell the truth. As for
corporate humility, it's not doing those
companies any favors.

I see both a bottom-line advantage and a save-the-world benefit to
trumpeting an honest green message. On the financial side, you're
able to market much more effectively to that vast market segment.

But even more to the point, you help make the world a better place.
Every time a company shares its green initiatives publicly, it shows

The Secret of Building a New Market Lies within these Five Simple Questions

If you've been struggling to build a green business, or to offer green products or services through an existing business, this column might just make your day—because I'm going to share the single biggest component of determining whether you will have a viable market for your offering.

All you have to do is ask yourself five simple questions:

1) What problem can you solve, or desire can you facilitate?

2) How is your method different from and better than existing solutions (what are the advantages, in other words)?

3) Who needs this problem solved strongly enough that they're willing to pay (who is the market)?

4) How do you reach those people?

5) How do you convince them to buy?

Let's see how this works out with a case study—an actual example I ran into recently.

Problem/Desire:

Thousands of gallons of water per household are wasted flushing small amounts of urine. An entrepreneur would like to help people save this water.

Possible Solutions:

There are several possible ways to fix this, such as composting toilets, graywater recycling (so that the water for flushing has already been used once, in a sink, dishwasher, shower, bath, or washing machine), and European-style two-way toilet switches that allow you to select a large flow for solids or a smaller flow for liquids. But this particular entrepreneur chose a different route: Go Flushless, an enzyme compound that elimates the odor and stain, allowing the urine to remain in the bowl with no ill effects.

Advantages:

Most of the other solutions involve extensive hardware modifications, and that's expensive. Go Flushless, by comparison, is cheap to buy and easy to implement (a couple of squirts on a standard hand-operated spray pump such as you'd use for window cleaner).

Possible Markets:

Green consumers who care about saving water are an obvious market—and because of the low point of entry, the product appeals not only to homeowners but also to renters. But there are several other markets, too.

Large consumers of water have economic reasons to save. Think about how much water is consumed in the bathrooms of sports stadiums, concert halls, schools, transportation terminals, and so forth. However, to reach this market, there would have to be a way to control the flush schedule remotely, which might be difficult in most circumstances (other than public urinals, some of which already use a timer instead of individual flush handles). So this would be a back-burner market, to pursue later once the technology catches up or the social expectations around flushing have shifted enough to create a space in the market within the society as a whole.

But there's another huge market that's much easier to reach: homeowners who live with septic systems and private water supplies (their own or a neighborhood well). Unlike the owners of large public bathrooms, this group has no technological or sociological challenges in implementing the Go Flushless method, and has a strong interest in conserving water so as to extend the lifespan of its infrastructure while decreasing the number of septic tank pumpouts.

Finally, there is another large market: people who live in places that face drought frequently, and where the culture has shifted in favor of flushing less—as it has in California, for example. Those folks are already letting the yellow stuff sit, and they would welcome a simple solution to the problem of odors and stains.

How to Reach these Markets:

These four different markets are going to congregate in different places.

For green consumers, exhibiting at a green festival makes a lot of sense. In fact, I met company owners Bill and Jane Monetti at a green festival where I was speaking and they were exhibiting—and selling quite a bit of their product.

Articles in trade magazines would effectively reach the industrial users. Homeowners with septic systems might best be reached through direct mail or even in-person sales calls. And people in drought-centric cultures could be reached simply enough by mass-market media such as radio, TV, and print newspapers.

And of course, although the message points would be different, it's important to note that the marketing techniques can transcend the barriers and reach every group. With different audience-specific messages, the Monettis could actively use social media, blogs, traditional media publicity, public speaking, product demonstrations, and their own website (no name a few examples).

Getting the Sale:

Target your appeals to each of these audiences. For green homeowners and tenants, saving water is enough of a reason. For the industrial bathroom owners as well as the well and septic crowd, a purely economic argument is going to work. And for those already not flushing because of drought, an appeal based on a clean, germ-free house and a toilet that is once again easy to clean should close the sale.

CISA: Matching Locavores and Local Farms

In the Pioneer Valley of Massachusetts (where I happen to live), you'll find a whole lot of farms with signage calling them "Local Heroes." You'll also see similar signs in grocery stores, supermarkets, farmers markets, plant nurseries, and even cafes and restaurants. And you'll see bumper stickers all over the region that say, "Be a Local Hero, Buy Locally Grown®."

Where did these signs come from, and what do they mean?

They came from an organization called Community Involved in Sustaining Agriculture, or CISA. And they signify that these farms are active partners in the local economy. People who want local foods seek them out, and buy from them. And these farms willingly sell to a

market that cuts out several of the middlemen and allows them to command a premium price. In an era when farms are facing huge challenges economically, the CISA member farms tend to be doing well.

Consumers get fresh foods (often picked that day)—and the knowledge that they're building the *local* economy. The money they spend with these farmers and their retailers comes back to the community in a myriad of ways: from support for sports teams and community causes to preserving open space for farmland as urban sprawl tries to encroach.

And farmers get ready markets—both wholesale and retail—of locals committed to the local economy, and of stores or food service establishments willing to facilitate that commitment by making the products available. Interestingly, some of the stores and restaurants that participate are not themselves locally based; a couple of very large chains are participating, selling local produce to local buyers even while they themselves are headquartered far away.

CISA was founded in 1993 as the Pioneer Valley Alliance for Sustainable Agriculture, and rebranded as an incorporated charitable organization in 1999, under its current name. Local Hero launched the same year. It offers many support resources and programs to local farmers, in addition to the Local Hero campaign: a farm share program for elders...market development among large institutions such as schools and hospitals...filling infrastructure needs such as processing centers...technical assistance to new farmers...workshops and instructional materials on marketing, grant writing, organic farming, and more...financing options...

But its public face is very much associated with the wildly popular Local Hero program. And through that program, a lot of dollars have shifted to local sources. In fact, according to Devon Whitney-Deal, CISA's Local

Hero Member Services Coordinator and one of nine employees, when the organization started tracking in 2003, there were only nine farmers markets in the Pioneer Valley—but now there are at least 40 seasonal markets plus four winter markets (a more than 400 percent increase in eight years). CISA has 199 member farmers, 50 retailers, 32 restaurants, and a total membership of 312. And in its three-county service area, reversing the farm-loss trend elsewhere, more acreage is actually in farmland now than when the group was founded.

In other words, through a massive branding campaign, this organization actually *created a consciousness about buying local.* People who in the past had not thought much about where their food comes from have made a conscious shift to buying some portion of their food supply from local sources—and that, in turn, has helped the farm economy to stay solvent.

The buy-local strategy, according to CISA's website, offers these five benefits (quoting):

- ✓ Keeps money in the local economy

- ✓ Preserves family farms

- ✓ Reduces oil-dependent transportation costs

- ✓ Protects our local landscapes

- ✓ Ensures that fresh, healthy food stays available and affordable to all

You won't find CISA on the web at cisa.com, .org, or .net; you have to look at buylocalfood.org/ (and what a great URL). I'm rather surprised that the organization hasn't started a franchise-like model on the website, like Craig's List. You'd kind of expect that by now there might be, for example, sydney.buylocalfood.org or kualalumpur.buylocalfood.org.

Whether the program uses a franchise model or not, I would think many communities around the world would be eagerly replicating this very successful program.

The Certification Conundrum

Everyone knows that third-party endorsement is a powerful credibility builder. This is especially true in the green movement, where so much of the marketing process is based on making a strong case that you have other values besides financial gain.

Certification is one way to gain that credibility. When an independent agency verifies that you are doing what you say you're doing, customer trust of you and your products go way up.

But certification raises a number of other issues:

What Does the Claim Actually Mean?

In the green marketplace, numerous products make all sorts of claims. The purchaser has to sort out what's really going on, and which claims are meaningful. Smart shoppers understand, for instance, that when a package says, "made with organic ingredients," that means as much as 30 percent of the product could be nonorganic. They don't yet have enough information to make an educated choice. What percentage of the ingredients are organic? Which ingredients were grown that way? The pesticide content of a nonfood product like nonorganic cotton will likely be much higher than the pesticide content of a fruit with edible skin, such as apples; all of this has to be factored into the buying decision. So this particular group will turn over the box and look at the ingredients list and look at which ingredients are really organic, and in what order the organic and nonorganic ingredients appear (thus, their relative predominance).

Self-Labeling Versus True Certification

Many labels claim a product is "natural" or "fairly traded"—but no standards exist for what is natural or fairly traded, and no certifying body regulates the claims. Consumers are at the mercy of the manufacturer and have to hope for honesty. By contrast, the word "organic" has a legal definition, and a neutral-party certification such as USDA Organic in the United States or Ecocert for European cosmetics gives it teeth. And various agencies such as the 26 members around the world of Fairtrade International (from Australia to the US) certify compliance with fair trade provisions: If you see those types of certifications, you know the claim was independently verified.

Retailers are also stepping into the breach. Whole Foods, for instance, now requires certification for any product claiming to be organic.

Of course in today's wired world, shoppers themselves can play a role in verifying claims. Social media allows anyone to accuse a company of making false claims, and to attract a wide audience; this is one of many reasons to be scrupulously honest in all your claims.

Space on the Label

Understanding the value of these certifications, some companies have paid for multiple certifications covering different aspects. For instance, I'm looking at a 3-ounce (66-gram) bar of Theo 91%-cocoa chocolate that bears the following certifications and claims:

✓ USDA Organic, certified by Washington State Department of Agriculture

✓ Fair For Life social and fair-trade certified by IMO

✓ Charity partner (Audubon, benefiting Costa Rican cacao farmers and bird habitat)

✓ Kosher

✓ 50% recycled packaging

✓ Vegan

Of the four ingredients, all four are noted as organic, and all but vanilla are also marked fair trade.

That's a lot of information, not even counting a big panel of text about the charity project. Imagine trying to fit all that on a 1-ounce (22-gram) package label.

On one hand, you want to take full advantage of all the work you've done to get those multiple certifications you painstakingly earned— and on the other hand, you still want to create an attractive package with adequate white space and a great design, not cluttered up with a bunch of certification logos.

If that were my challenge, I might put text like this on the wrapper:

"Certified organic, fair trade, kosher and vegan. Benefits Audubon's forest, farm, and bird preservation efforts in Costa Rica. For more details, please scan this QR code into your smartphone, or visit www._____."

That way, you get all the good stuff out front, provide two ways for people who want all the details to get them—including the instant gratification made possible by the QR code—and still keep plenty of room on the label.

Why Greens Hate Hard–Sell

Imagine going down the road in your eco-friendly hybrid car (or better yet, your public transit conveyance or your bicycle), listening to some earnest musician's song about global warming. All of a sudden, this commercial is screaming at you:

Go green today! Act NOW to lock in your savings! Call 800-555-CASH or visit www.CashBackEnergySavings.com. That's 800-555-CASH or www.CashBackEnergySavings.com (note: phone and URL are fictional.

How do you feel about this loud, intrusive interruption?

Guess what—that's exactly how your prospects feel when they encounter hypey, in-your-face green marketing. And they tune it out. In fact, even well outside the green sector, obnoxious marketing is a lot less effective than it used to be. We have hundreds of thousands of sources for information now, and when one of them gets annoying, we leave.

Yes, there are companies out there doing this sort of thing—but no, it doesn't work very well.

Even more than the public as a whole, most segments of the green market are turned off by screamy hype. People who are drawn to green products and green lifestyles perceive themselves as thoughtful and intelligent, sorting out a range of competing (and sometimes conflicting) benefits and demerits to make choices that are good for the earth, and also good for themselves, their family, and their wallets.

And they are hungry for tools that help them make those decisions. They will demand that you provide the information they need in order to thoroughly evaluate for themselves whether your claims make sense and whether your offering is right for them. They will spend time reading articles, poring over back pages of websites, checking out your endorsements and testimonials, watching informational videos, scanning social media and blog feeds...and, especially, discussing planned major purchases with a cadre of trusted friends and associates.

To make it even more challenging, different sectors within that great big green market will bring different motivations and needs, and respond differently to the same marketing.

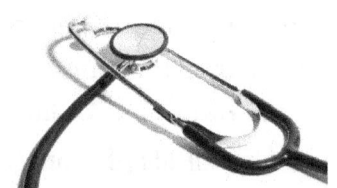

Let's look at one hypothetical typical green family. Children's health may be the primary concern of the mom, while her husband worries about the soaring cost of heating their home. His mother, who lives with them, has poor circulation and is cold all the time. The teenage daughter wants to make sure the workers involved are paid fair wages for harvesting the crops, but her younger brother is trying to find organic food that tastes good and doesn't seem weird to his classmates. If you try to reach all of these very different constituencies with the same marketing message, all of them will ignore you.

One way around that is to do different marketing pieces for each segment; Volkswagen and Apple are two companies that have always done that pretty well. Apple, for instance, markets one set of benefits to graphic artists, a different set to educators, and entirely different ones for musicians and film production people.

But for smaller companies, that approach may be expensive. A better alternative might be to *incorporate multiple marketing messages into the same communication.* Offer multiple pages on a website or brochure, multiple sections in a retail store, different series of informational documents aimed at different audiences.

For instance, a manufacturer of energy-efficient window quilts might create a website landing page offering the option to click to separate pages for high-end builders (looking for luxury features to differentiate their houses from others), interior designers (all about style), landlords (concerned with cost and appearance, and homeowners (balancing savings, durability, and their fashion statement). And those pages, in turn can subdivide by other interest areas.

Or, going back to our imaginary family, the company can market not only by professional affiliation but also by the particular interest. So a landing page might have links with titles like:

- ✓ How our window quilts can keep your family healthy and lower your medical bills (the mom will read that one)

✓ Why you're probably throwing away up to $800 every winter—through your windows (dad)

✓ The inside story of why we use only fair-trade cotton and how it's working miracles in the farming villages where we work (daughter)

✓ Looking to have the coolest room in town? Check out these awesome designs (son)

✓ How to stay nice and cozy-warm this winter without putting on a second and third sweater (that page is for grandma)

Next month, we'll look at the one of the best kinds of non-hype marketing: positioning yourself as the knowledgeable, helpful expert.

Build Your Expert Reputation, and Let Customers Come to You

Last month, we discussed why hypey, in-your-face marketing doesn't work for the green market, and looked at how to segment your marketing messages for different audiences. This month, let's take it a step further, and look at one of the most powerful (and least expensive) of all marketing methods: providing helpful, useful, actionable information that leads your prospect to consider you not only the expert, but the go-to company when they need what you do.

There are dozens of way to do this. You'll want to find the ones that are in tune with your audience's preferences and tastes. A few examples:

- ✓ Get in front of your best prospects as a speaker.

- ✓ Teach an ongoing course.

- ✓ Lead or be a featured guest on expert teleseminars, webinars, and chats.

- ✓ Join some Internet communities in your field of interest, and participate helpfully, answering questions and giving advice (this single strategy did more to turn my own business from a tiny consulting practice serving my own local area to the successful international business it is today).

✓ Prepare a series of White Papers or special reports illuminating certain confusing aspects of your industry and helping people make good decisions.

✓ Conduct a survey and release the results to major and trade media with some juicy summing-up quotes.

✓ Become a published author—publishing a book makes you an automatic expert, impresses a whole lot of people, and is much easier than it used to be.

✓ Get quoted in major media—not as hard as you may think—and then send the clips or links to your prospects.

✓ Create and distribute your own e-zine or printed newsletter (e-zine is greener and cheaper, but in some situations, print may be more effective)—and then later repurpose these articles by placing them on article banks such as ezinearticles.com or ideamarketers.com (if you have enough of these articles, and they categorize neatly, you can even turn them into a book later).

✓ Write your own blog and post to it at least twice a week (more is better).

- ✓ Be a guest blogger or columnist for other people's publications, including high–status expert sites like Examiner.com, Ask.com, and Triple Pundit.com.

- ✓ Share great articles, postcasts, studies, and other resources in your field on social media such as Twitter, Google+, LinkedIn, and Facebook (two tips: First, no more than 10 to 20 percent of these resources should point to your own stuff—and second, software tools can automate some of this, for example automatically feeding your blog into your Facebook business page and LinkedIn profile).

Since the green market really craves information, as we discussed last month, you're actually doing your prospects a service by providing access to the information they seek. Provide the information, answers their questions, help them solve a problem or meet a need—and do it all with a friendly and approachable tone. And then it probably won't be long before your prospects start coming to you and saying things like, "I really enjoyed your article in Green Business Daily. Do you ever consult individually with retail stores? I'd like to hire you."

While old-fashioned push marketing is intrusive and even offensive, nobody gets offended when you simply place pertinent, helpful, well-written information in front of your prospects: information that's easy to access, easy to understand, and easy to implement.

What you're actually doing is creating a relationship and marketing based on that relationship. You build trust, confidence, and a sense that you can help with their problems or goals. And instead of going for the quick hit and expecting people to take action on the basis of interrupting them, you become a presence over time, showing up pleasurably in their mailboxes and social networks, and at the green conferences and trade shows they attend.

Another advantage is that unlike push marketers who have to pay to place their ads, you are reaching your prospects for free, and sometimes even getting paid to do your own marketing.

If you'd like help developing this type of marketing, don't be afraid to get in touch. I'm blessed that I actually enjoy strategizing on the best types of relationship marketing for you, and writing these kinds of materials.

The WIIFM Factor and Green Marketing

When marketing green products and services to an eco-conscious audience, the most important question may be "How does this help the planet?"

But if you also want to reach people who are not committed greens, the most important question for them will be "What's in it for me?"

In the marketing world, "What's in it for me?" is often abbreviated as WIIFM. And since in the eastern half of the United States, radio station names are usually a group of four letters beginning with W—though some stations have three or five characters, some marketers joke that WIIFM is your prospect's "favorite radio station"—and you have to tune in if you want the sale.

Most of the time, you will want your marketing to reach both green and non-green markets—so that means you should be answering both questions, and answering them well. You want your marketing to convince these prospects that they and the planet will both be better off dealing with you and buying your offerings.

In other words, you want to combine planetary interest with self-interest.

That means, you might have to focus on such attributes as...

✓ The "cool" factor (a rooftop hydroponic garden, a sleek stainless steel reusable water bottle)

✓ Luxury or sportiness (how about the Tesla roadster, an electric car that looks like a Ferrari)

✓ Saving money (two-sided printers can save you about 40 percent of your paper costs)

✓ Comfort (better insulation or a much more efficient heating/air conditioning system means an end to cold and drafty winter nights, and some relief from sweltering summer days)

✓ Better health while getting close to nature (walking or running shoes, bicycles)

✓ Better health through avoiding toxics (natural cleaning and personal care products, organic clothing)

✓ Helping businesses and individuals comply with tighter laws and regulations, and to cover new areas such as Cradle-to-Cradle waste recovery; products and services that keep materials out of the waste stream, eliminate harmful chemicals, or reduce water and energy use will grow in popularit)

✓ Higher quality (buying local organic fruits and veggies and other gourmet foods from a farmers market, specialty store, or Community Supported Agriculture farm—once you've tasted the incredible burst of flavor from a locally grown, vine-ripened tomato, a hand-crafted cheese, or even a small-

batch brewery beer, you may not ever want to buy
the poor imitations at the supermarket)

How green is your customer? Outside of the super-green product arena where people really do make their purchase decisions to help the world (and are even willing to pay extra to get it), most people are going to fall somewhere in the middle of a continuum. Many people will buy a green offering if it's comparable in price, quality, and convenience, but won't pay much extra or incur extra hassle. If it's better than the conventional alternative, the sale is even easier.

Thus, if you can show that your t-shirts made from recycled soda bottles are at least as comfortable, durable, and affordable as a conventional non-organic cotton t-shirt, you should get the sale.

If you can show how your architect and your construction company can build a house so well insulated it doesn't need a furnace or air conditioner, using the savings to cover the cost of the energy improvements, you should get the sale

Combining self-interest with planetary interest means your marketing not only reaches both the green and non-green audiences, but it reaches them with both messages at the same time.

And thus, they will appeal strongly to people the audiences all along that continuum:

✓ Deep greens who feel guilty unless they can make
an environmentally friendly choice

- ✓ People who are willing to go green, but not willing to inconvenience themselves (these are the folks in the middle)

- ✓ Those who don't care about green and may even be hostile, but recognize the superiority of your product

Once you've gone green while maintaining or increasing those qualities your buyers seek, your next job is to create marketing that tells that story, shows how your product or service is the most sensible and most exciting choice. (You'll find a lot of advice on that in my latest book, Guerrilla Marketing Goes Green.)

Going Global, Part 1: Brand Identity in a Global Economy

What's the first thing that comes into your head when someone says "Mercedes"?

If you're in Europe, I'll guess that you think of a company that has a car, truck, or bus for every market niche. In the United States— where General Motors, Ford, and Chrysler own that positioning— Mercedes brings up images of high-end sport and luxury cars; its competitors are companies like Porsche and Rolls-Royce, not Chevrolet or Dodge. (Ironically, Chrysler was actually owned by Mercedes' parent company, Daimler, from 1988-2007.) And in many other parts of the world, Mercedes is the workhorse of taxi, truck and bus fleets, supplying durable vehicles at affordable cost. In the Spanish-speaking world, Mercedes is also a popular female name, for which the car was named more than 100 years ago.

In short, the same brand has very different associations in different parts of the world. And this works in the green world, too: What's the first thing that comes into your head when someone says "Vitasoy"?

As a green business owner, you might be into natural foods—and you could know Vitasoy as a brand of organic soymilk, with various flavor options and a health consciousness. You might even know that the company owns several other soy-related brands, including Nasoya and Azumaya tofu products in the US and Unicurd in Singapore.

But in cultures like China, Hong Kong, and Latin America, their soymilks—under such names as Calci-Plus, Tsing Sum Zhan, and San Sui—are marketed as mainstream household beverages; packages I've seen in Latin American markets do not mention the word "organic."

Vitasoy's milk is called Soy Milky in Australia—a name that would not go over well in the United States.

In short, the same company has very different associations and very different product lines in different parts of the world.

Let's stay with green foods for another example: natural breakfast cereals. To a shopper in the United Kingdom, Weetabix® is a well-known and diverse line of cereals: the regular kind that's similar to shredded wheat...organic, crispy minis with chocolate, strawberries, peanut butter, or fruit and nuts...baked with golden syrup...chocolate (non-mini)...crunchy bran...and then variations made with different grains, such as Oatabix. There's even an o-shaped imitation of Cheerios. But in the US, it's unusual to see anything other than the basic biscuits, sold as a green product.

What's the point? It's that large companies—in the green world or in the general consumer marketplace—go after different markets, and market differently, in different parts of the world, or in different market segments within the same country.

In fact, smart companies segment much more closely than by country. Within 16 kilometers (10 miles) of my house, the same supermarket chain has stores in four communities. Walking the aisles, you'd think they were different companies entirely. Two are geared toward the adventurous tastes of healthy-living folks in the nearby college towns, with a lot of natural products, green packaging, exotic local fruits and vegetables, and so on. And one of those, in a more international community, has an Asian foods section that's bigger than some Asian grocery stores. The third, in a heavily Hispanic city, has a product selection geared to Puerto Rican tastes.

 And the fourth, in a working-class city that hosts a large military base, is the land of packaged, bland convenience foods for a burger-and-pasta-salad crowd. It would be hard to find anything organic on that store's shelves.

You'll find examples of this kind of segmentation in industry after industry. Even something like book cover design will be startlingly different for the same book in different parts of the world.

If you read this column, you're probably not a giant multinational company with resources to create different product variations all over the world.

But these days, all of us are global businesses. As a green marketing consultant and copywriter working solo from a farmhouse in the northeastern United States, I've not only served clients from all parts of my own country, but also all across Asia and Europe: Japan, Cyprus, Israel, England, France, Germany, Belgium, and elsewhere. And this column runs in Australia and Asia, as well as in the United States.

If an international client comes to me to reach the green market in the United States, that's easy for me. But if that client wants to reach an audience in a different market, I have to find ways to put myself in the mindset of a potential customer who thinks very differently from me, and that can be a challenge.

For me, the way around this is to focus on the slices of the market that play to my core strengths. For instance, if a company wants to reach the green consumer, or market green products and services to either green or nongreen audiences, my subject knowledge is strong enough to make up for the cultural differences.

If you want to go into different markets, ask yourself questions like these:

- ✓ What do you offer that a customer can't find at home already?

- ✓ How will you deal with shipping, customs, and tariff costs, and will you be able to compete after factoring those in?

- ✓ Who will sell and service your products in that country?

- ✓ How might a tweak in the product, packaging, or marketing make it more attractive in that market?

✓ How does entering this far-away market make the world better or address environmental and social problems—and how can you use that commitment in your marketing?

Good luck! And if you need guidance on this journey, feel free to contact me.

Going Global, Part 2: Creating Positioning for Global Brands

Last month, we looked at when it might make sense to enter a global market with your green product or service. This month, we'll take a look at market positioning that might make it worth the hassle and expense of entering new countries.

Your Unique Selling Proposition, or USP, is marketing-speak for the factor that makes your offering special enough to win over buyers who either have been meeting the need elsewhere or didn't realize they needed your product or service. If you're entering a different country, your USP will have to be clear and convincing enough that people will switch.

In the world of green products and services, you'll construct your USP based in either or both of two different themes: how the product or service improves your customer's life (solves a problem, meets a need, fulfills a desire)—and how it helps others and the world. While customers who already think green are receptive to the second, to reach people other than committed greens, you also need positioning points in the first category.

A few possibilities:

Higher Standards

I've been amazed for several years that European cosmetics and personal care product companies haven't stormed the US with an appeal to consumer safety, i.e., "Because we're based in Spain, we have to meet European Union standards for product safety. These standards are much tougher than those in the United States, and that's your guarantee that our shampoos are safe and healthy for your children." This is a market opportunity waiting to be captured, and the early movers could have quite a leg up, particularly following the scares about safety issues in imported Chinese goods. Yet even European companies like The Body Shop that do have a presence in the US fail to capitalize on this in their marketing.

Standards in health, the environment (organic, biodegradable packaging, waste recapture, no animal testing, etc.), ease of use, etc. all make great positioning points.

Economic Opportunity for the Poor

If, say, your product is sourced from organic biodynamic fair-trade ingredients, that gives you bragging rights. While many consumers around the world recognize that fair trade, organic, and biodynamic are good things, they may not recognize exactly what it means. You, as the product manufacturer, importer, or marketer, must educate them. Your customers and prospects need to know that buying from you means not only a living wage to the farmer, but also:

Certification that child slaves are not used (an especially big issue in the cocoa industry)

A pool of money to the village cooperative, which uses it for democratically decided improvement projects such as building wells—and that in turn means teenage girls are able to stay in school because they're not spending half the day carrying pitchers of water several miles

Money that stays in the local producer communities and is not  sucked away to the developed world by giant corporations

Sustainable farming practices that mean the harvest will continue for many years, because the soil is nurtured, not depleted, and the farms use companion planting rather than destructive monocropping

The consumer is spared exposure to harmful chemicals, and gets to savor a food product that still contains its original nutrients and thus offers both higher nutritional content and better flavor

When you present things this way, you provide good reasons to buy from you instead of some commoditized agribusiness firm. Wouldn't any smart consumer want to make a choice like that?

And there are other types of appeals on social-betterment grounds. Companies like Khaya Cookies in South Africa <www.khayacookies.com/> or Greyston Bakery in the United States <www.greystonbakery.com/> make a big point of providing jobs to people who would otherwise be unemployable: young mothers in the townships outside Johannesburg, and ex-offenders or people with mental disabilities from the slums of New York, respectively.

Deeper Environmental Benefits

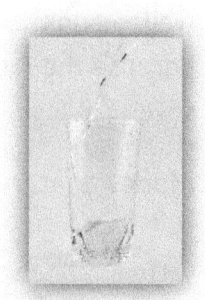

What do your green attributes *really* mean? Less intensive use of water, energy or materials and reduced or recaptured waste output can mean lower prices to the consumer, reduced contribution to catastrophic climate change, more productive farmland, etc. Are these important enough to get consumers to switch from a home-country brand to your export? And will the differences make up for the environmental impact of shipping something halfway across the world?

The Key Concept: Make Your Story Meaningful

When you bring a product to market in a different country, the marketing challenge is to tell "the story behind the story"—to make it come alive with your commitment to a better world that is so strong it has brought you all the way across an ocean to do business. This kind of marketing is a good thing even in the domestic market, but with the extra challenges of going global, it's crucial. Keep asking, "what does this mean? Why is it important? Why should my customer care?"

And once again, you don't have to go it alone. People like me are happy to help you succeed.

Publicity, Part 1: Should You Seek Mainstream Media Publicity for Your Green Business?

 Publicity uses traditional and new media—such as newspapers, magazines, newsletters, blogs, radio, podcasts, and television—to get the word out about your product, service, and/or ideas—not by paying for advertising, but by becoming part of the content.

There are many ways to get media publicity. Examples include (among many others) an article about your product or service, or that at least mentions you, in either the news or feature pages...a profile of your business...an announcement of an event you're doing...an interview with you on TV or radio...a reporter covering your product launch press conference. It brings visibility, credibility, opportunity, and sales.

Publicity provides the seal of approval of a trusted outside source: a journalist. Like testimonials and awards, this third-party validation helps you stand out in a crowded marketplace. And of course, it also means that a lot more people hear about you. Not only will people see the newscast, read the publication, or hear you on the radio, but in many cases you can quote from the publicity in your own marketing materials, link to it on your website, and generally maximize the impact to your benefit.

Put yourself in your prospect's shoes for a moment: if you're trying to choose a vendor, and you visit one website that shows the product has been covered in the Sydney Morning Herald in Australia, the Business Times in Kuala Lumpur, Malaysia, and the Boston Globe in the United States—but the other websites you visit don't mention any press—which are you more likely to choose?

The Tradeoff: Credibility vs. Control

When you get free publicity rather than pay for advertising, you give up control over the content. The news media can write what they want, and you may have to deal with correcting inaccuracies later. But you have the added legitimacy of being chosen to represent your field.

And because news coverage at least pretends to be unbiased, it is more valuable than advertising; you get, in a sense, a testimonial—a disinterested, credible party who thinks you're worthy of positive attention. Many people take news coverage more seriously than advertising—and may be more likely to be influenced by it than by a paid ad. This is particularly true these days, as ads not only have less credibility than they used to, but are often bypassed entirely, as new technologies allow them to be skipped.

For green businesses, publicity has many additional advantages:

- ✓ Publicity helps you introduce complex concepts to new audiences. If, for instance, you run a zero-waste factory, or build homes that don't need a furnace or air conditioning system, a good article can make it clear that these "impossible" achievements are actually quite possible.

✓ News coverage educates the public about environmental issues. From climate change to recycling, the press helps citizens understand the wider issues, and how they play out locally.

✓ When you tell your story in the news media, you can differentiate your business from not-so-green competitors.

✓ And sometimes, publicity leads to more contacts that advance your career: a company president sees the article and decides you're the perfect consultant to transition that company to renewable energy and green manufacturing...a meeting planner contacts you to see whether you could speak at a conference in front of 200 of your best prospects...a different journalist sees the story and wants to cover you as well. In short, the media coverage can become a doorway to far more lucrative ventures.

Oh yes, and don't forget that every now and then, an article or a TV or radio interview can actually motivate people to go out and buy your product then and there! Especially if you make it easy by including your website, your phone number and some kind of special offer.

Publicity, Part 2: What Kinds of Messages Can Bring You Mainstream Media Publicity?

We touched very lightly last month on the types of activity that can bring you coverage in traditional media. This month, we'll go into more detail, and then next month, I'll share resources that help you get coverage.

First of all, if what you know about news-worthy activities is more than five years old, the very first thing you need to do is update your knowledge. In the not-so-distant past, activities like publishing a book or CD, launching a new website, introducing a new 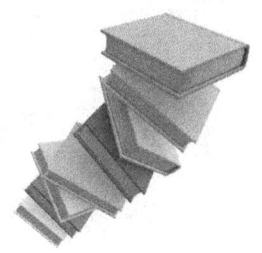 product, or speaking at a minor conference were often enough to get coverage—but not anymore.

In today's world of short attention spans, information bombardment, and a news system that focuses on drama and celebrity much more than on life-changing developments in science and technology or even on the real issues that modern nations face, those types of accomplishments are not enough anymore. For example, tens of millions of books are published every year—and that means it's a lot harder to get publicity for a new book than it was 20 years ago, when the worldwide total was probably under a million (42,217 books were published just in the United States in 1993, compared with more than 3 million in 2010). So if you've written a book about zero-waste manufacturing, it won't be enough anymore to send your local newspaper a press release with the headline, "Green Manufacturing Expert Publishes New Book." Reporters keep their fingers right near the delete key as they scan hundreds of press releases arriving in their inboxes, and that one won't make the cut.

In today's world, you have to be much more effective in telling your green story: *you have to think like a journalist!* And an overwhelmed journalist with a supercrowded inbox and four stories to research and write on a typical work day, at that.

Journalists are looking at what sells newspapers, cable TV accounts, and radio ads. They look at their readers' pain points, problems, aspirations, and goals—even better if there's a tie-in with hot news stories or celebrities.

So you must market your green products and services the same way. Focus on the problems you solve, the benefits your customers achieve, or the entertainment value you create—along with your credibility. Thus, a better headline would be something like "Manufacturers Can Slash Disposal Costs by 80 Percent While Opening New Markets, Bestselling Author Claims." That's a headline that will make a business journalist want to read more.

Similarly, if your CEO makes a speech at a conference, focus on the message within the speech; if a reporter sees a headline like "ExxonMobil CEO: Climate Change is the Most Crucial Issue of Our

Time," it's going to get a lot more attention than "Oil Company Executive Addresses Conference of Drill Bit Dealers." (That example is completely hypothetical—but I would love to read in the press about a major oil company's commitment to addressing climate change—particularly ExxonMobil, which has funded many studies that question climate change.)

So here are some results-focused "pegs" that you can use to convert your publicity outreach into news coverage, even for the sorts of events that are no longer news by themselves:

- ✓ Solving one or more problems

- ✓ Producing benefits not just to customers but to other stakeholders (for instance, the benefit of Fair Trade food products is the economic boost to the producer community, which in turn becomes more able to buy other goods and services)

- ✓ Achieving and quantifying a major green milestone such as 60 percent reduced emissions or 100-percent–recycled raw materials

- ✓ Setting a major environmental goal or policy statement, especially one that the mainstream business world would consider difficult or impossible

- ✓ Creating a whole new product category (very common in the green market: an enzyme that means you don't have to flush as often, a vertical garden space for apartment dwellers, a wheelchair

transporter no bigger than a Smart or a Fiat 500, to
name three actual products)

And if you have trouble thinking up creative, benefit-driven news
pegs, don't be afraid to call in an expert. Lots of people, including
me, can write a terrific press release for you.

Publicity, Part 3: How to Get Publicity

Imagine for a moment that you get your hometown newspaper, open up the business page, and are happily stunned to see a big article about you and your work.

Now imagine that it's not your hometown newspaper—it's actually 5000 miles/8000 kilometers away from where you live.

Thrilled? You should be! I certainly was when I saw this photo, featuring my book cover in an article about my ideas and the talk I was doing the following week.

I've been similarly thrilled to see "my name in lights" in such places as the New York Times, the Wall Street Journal, Entrepreneur Magazine, and even Woman's Day, each of which have cited me multiple times. And even more thrilled to see coverage around the world...in major publications in Australia, Romania, Colombia, and elsewhere. I even had my book cover blasted across an electronic billboard in New York's Times Square. And I'm especially thrilled since none of this media attention cost me even one penny.

It also gladdens my heart that when I get this kind of coverage, it means more people are learning that green and ethical business can be profitable business—that all of us, together, are creating a new, earth-centered business paradigm. And it doesn't hurt that my high media visibility sometimes brings in a new client or speaking invitation.

In a typical year, I do 50 to 150 interviews in print, Internet, and broadcast media. I do this without a public relations agency, and without a corporate presence; I am simply one solopreneur working from a farmhouse in a rural area.

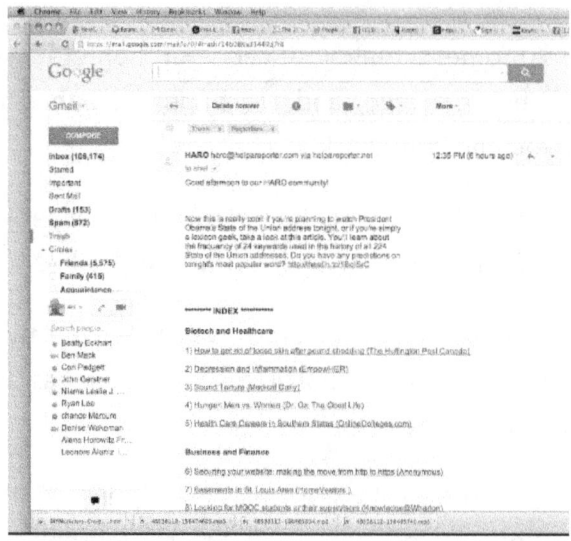

HARO (Help A Reporter Out) www.helpareporter.com
(the above screenshot shows part of a HARO table of contents)

Would you like to get free exposure for your business? It's not that hard.

We talked about press releases earlier in this series. The Kauai writeup came from a press release sent by the meeting organizer who brought me in.

But there's an even better way to get in front of reporters: *offer to be a source for reporters who are already looking for story sources for a specific article.* Conveniently, there are several no-cost services that match reporters looking for sources with sources seeking coverage:

- ✓ HARO (Help A Reporter Out):
  www.helpareporter.com

- ✓ Reporter Connection:
  www.ReporterConnection.com

- ✓ Pitch Rate: www.PitchRate.com

- ✓ Radio Guest List: www.RadioGuestList.com

Sign up for some or all of these, follow the Twitter feeds of @helpareporter, @reporterconxn, @pitchrate, @profnet, @prleads, and @radioguestlist—and pitch when you match the criteria the reporter requests (DON'T spam them with inappropriate responses, unless you want to get banned).

Now, some pitching hints to turn queries into coverage:

- ✓ Respond as instantly as possible (except for Radio GuestList—in most cases, the radio producers have an ongoing need, and you'll stand out more by waiting a week or two until the deluge dies down). These queries may draw 200 responses, so the fastest in get the closest consideration. Consider setting up a separate e-mail address to receive and respond to queries, and check that account every hour from 6 a.m. to 6 pm. US Eastern Time (or better yet, turn on audio notification just for that account).

✓ Stay on topic and relevant—don't try to make a fit where one doesn't really exist. That means paying attention to such factors as geographic needs, size of company, or anything else the reporter might specify in the query (yeah, it would be nice if more reporters put the restrictions in the headline).

✓ Give the reporter something to quote right in your query (I usually do between 2–5 bullet points or one very meaty paragraph).

✓ Mention your relevant credentials and include a link to your media room on your website.

✓ Set up Google and Yahoo Alerts for your name, book title, and perhaps main topic keywords (if not too general), so you can see if you get quoted—reporters won't always tell you.

What goes in a media room? Anything a reporter might find useful in researching a story, such as photos for reprint, a list of media that have covered you, press releases, a bio, and—very important for radio or TV—sample interview questions. You can see one of my media rooms at http://greenandprofitable.com/contact/media-room/#media —you're welcome to use it as a model.

Publicity, Part 4:
But Social Media is Different:
10 Social Media Marketing
Success Principles

Just as marketing through free publicity is different than marketing via paid advertising or your own channels, marketing on social media—sites like Twitter, Facebook, LinkedIn, and Pinterest—is different as well. I could easily put together a list of 100 tips, but let's keep it simple and just do ten.

1. See the Big Picture

Social media provides a powerful toolkit to change the discourse—so instead of wasting space on what you ate for breakfast, post content designed to influence other people (Facebook-style visual memes, even if they're nothing but quotes, are great for this). At the same time, remember to be human. Show some parts of your personality, mention your own life events, and offer congrats or condolences when you have the chance.

2. Skip the Hard-Sell

Avoid skewing toward blatant "buy my stuff" self-promotion—unless you want 90% of your followers to leave and the remaining 10% to be spambots. I recommend no more than 1 totally self-promotional post every 20 posts.

3. Your Posts Live Forever

Social media is a *permanent* record. Never post anything that will embarrass you later; drunken-idiot pictures may be fun at the party, but don't look so good when college turns into job-application time. Even if you go back and delete a post, it could come back to haunt you, because the content will still be accessible to people who know how to hunt for it.

4. Small is Beautiful

Even Twitter's 140 characters is plenty if you combine a compelling headline with a link to the full article and/or post a picture.

5. The Social Media Success Formula

You need two things to succeed in social media: content...and audience! Content is the easy part. If you want people to follow you, go out and build an audience, *organically*. You do this by following people of influence, interacting with them, sharing their posts, commenting (appropriately—this is NOT an invitation to spam) not just on their social media but on their blogs, commenting on the comments made about your own posts, sharing your lists of people to follow, etc.

6. Understand Social Media's Strengths and Limitations

The power of social media is the way messages can spread to friends of friends of friends—people you couldn't have reached directly. Some of them will start following you; some you can engage in dialog with. But the flaw of social media is the way you often don't see the same people consistently, and who you do see is very arbitrary depending on when you happen to sign on. Tools like HootSuite or TweetDeck provide partial fixes; for instance, they allow you to set up a column that tracks people you want to follow more closely. Also use a social media tool to schedule your posts for maximum impact, autopost to social media every time you put up a new blog post, and post to more than one network with a couple of clicks.

7. The "Secret Sauce" of Mainstream Social Media

Participation in subcommunities such as LinkedIn groups and Facebook pages is another way to overcome this limitation. Pick two or three that reach at least 500 of your best prospects, have high discussion quality, and a good number of people actively participating

8. The Even Bigger Secret—Back from the 1990s

Similarly, find some old-style email-based discussion lists (for example, on yahoogroups.com); these are much less popular than they used to be, but they put you in front of the same audience of prime prospects over and over again, and usually allow you to include at least a short email signature that includes a slogan, link to your website, and your contact information.

9. Bring Them Back to You

Let social media work in tandem with media you control; do not let social media platforms exclusively own your best content; draw people to something where the rug can't be pulled out from under you, such as a blog on your own domain.

10. Keep the Content Alive

Remember that only a tiny fraction of your followers/friends will see any particular post. So don't be afraid to post the content again—but word it differently, and have several other posts in between, so you don't look like an a-hole if someone goes to your profile page. On Facebook, you can also keep your important posts in other people's streams longer (with this week's algorithms, anyway) by going back and commenting on them—so have a dialog with the people who comment on your post, but maybe an hour or so later.

Convince on Climate Change with Nonenvironmental Arguments

Recently, the UK newspaper The Guardian argued that activists could get more traction with nongreens on climate change by pointing out the public health consequences of failing to act.[1]

And that's certainly true—but it's nowhere near the whole story.

Over a year ago, in my April, 2012 column, I wrote about marketing green products to nongreen audiences. I talked about finding the what's-in-it-for-me factor so that nongreens want to buy green products because they're  more hip, or cheaper, or more luxurious, etc. And I've been pointing this out in my Making Green Sexy talks for at least three years.

Now we have to take that same way of thinking and shift it from the material world—products and services—to the less tangible realm of

---

1 http://www.guardian.co.uk/sustainable-business/climate-change-environment-health-problem

what kind of world they want to live in, what kind of world they want to leave to their children and grandchildren.

Because these folks don't generally consider human impact on the earth, save-the-planet arguments won't carry much water with them.

But we can gain converts to the clause of reversing catastrophic climate change on several grounds that are not blatant appeals to environmentalism, among them:

- ✓ Economics

- ✓ Health (as The Guardian pointed out)

- ✓ Lifestyle

- ✓ Let's look at each of these in turn.

Economics

The longer we wait to reverse catastrophic climate change, the more expensive it will be. I could fill this entire column with numerous economic arguments for addressing climate change NOW, and still only scratch the surface. Here are a few positive-focused and negative-focused arguments:

- ✓ Avoiding the enormous costs of cleaning up after climate–change–related storms like Hurricanes Katrina, Rita, Irene, and Sandy (many trillions of dollars)—and after messy oil spills like Exxon Valdez and BP Deepwater Horizon

- ✓ Switching to clean, renewable energy sources stops the transfer of wealth from individual consumers to oil barons and big banks, and from industrialized nations to countries that can be hostile to the modern world

- ✓ Saying goodbye to paying energy bills, because you can harness free energy from the sun, wind, tides, etc.

- ✓ Keeping global temperatures where they belong means lower costs for air conditioning and heating.

- ✓ Paying lower taxes if we no longer need the military to secure fossil fuel sources

Health

- ✓ Getting off coal will reduce asthma, emphysema, and other breathing diseases.

- ✓ Too much heat is a public health issue. Remember the summer of 2003, when thousands of people died in Europe's heat wave?

- ✓ Natural gas fracking and tar sands oil extraction put our water supply at severe risk. Water pollution ruins not just our drinking water but also water for agriculture, medicine, food packaging, etc.

Lifestyle

✓ Transporting ourselves by bicycle or on our own two feet offers the benefits of cardiovascular exercise: appropriate weight, fitness, increased endurance, longevity, etc. If that's not practical, using mass transit at least converts stressy driving time to time you can do something non-stressful and enjoyable, like read a book or watch a movie.

✓ Crops or animals that depend on cold weather, like maple syrup or polar bears, are at risk if it doesn't get cold enough. At the same time, pests like mosquitoes and ticks will provide year-round misery without a frost to kill them off for the winter.

✓ We all feel happier when we base more of our diet on local, sustainable foods. It's not just that they have less of a carbon footprint because they don't have to be transported great distances. The arguments that will persuade nongreens are how much better they taste, how many more nutrients are accessible in really fresh foods, and—among the more forward-thinking—how much more of a boost buying local provides to the local economy.

There are probably several other categories of talking points where greens can reach out to nongreens. In all of it, we need to focus on the direct benefits to the people we're talking about, who may not be committed greens. To put it another way, we need to reach each person with the arguments that resonate with that specific person.

Let's all go out and convince a few people!

[1]. *http://www.guardian.co.uk/sustainable-business/climate-change-environment-health-problem*

If You've Gone Green—
Remember to Brag

Looking out over the fields of the farm I live on, I always smile when I see our luscious organic garden. Once, when we had a particularly bountiful harvest of hot peppers, I went to the garden, picked five pounds of surplus, and brought the whole big bag to my neighbors' farmstand. They sell produce from a bunch of local farms, usually labeled with the farm of origin and the town, and of course, the price.

So I was figuring mine would go out with something like "Grown right here on this farm by our neighbors, with no pesticides or chemical fertilizers" and the price per pound. (They couldn't legally call our homegrown veggies organic, because for our home garden, we don't go through any certification process.) With a sign like that, I would have expected my chiles to go flying out the door, and I would have had a steady market for the remaining two months of the season.

That was the theory. But for some reason, instead of displaying them proudly at the front of the store with the rest of the local vegetables, instead of trumpeting their purity and hyperlocalism, they put my beautiful peppers in an out-of-the-way spot, with no sign at all. And there, they slowly shriveled over the next week or so. Needless to say, I didn't bring them any more to sell.

Here are the two marketing lessons the farmstand forgot:

- ✓ When your product or service has attributes that are demonstrably superior, announce those attributes to the world. As it happens, our area has a very strong awareness about the importance of buying local foods and the superiority of fresh/local/organic. And the farmstand, located in a rural area close to three college towns, caters to this educated market with a wide range of local and fair trade products. Failing to label my peppers was an act of self-sabotage, because this aware demographic had no idea what made the peppers special, and therefore they didn't choose to purchase them. After all, if your sets of benefits don't convince you that you have a better offering, why will they convince anyone else?

- ✓ Make it easy for your customers to get the information they need. Failing to put a price on the display meant that anyone considering the peppers would have to go to the counter and ask—and that extra step is a disincentive.

A less personal example: I know of a household paper products company that began making its paper products from recycled raw materials all the way back in 1950. When Earth Day first happened back in 1970 and society began to be much more conscious of environmental issues, this company was perfectly placed to capitalize on the rapidly growing trend by pointing out that they had switched to recycled paper 20 years earlier.

Unfortunately, that thought apparently did not occur to them, and certainly they didn't put it into action. It was about 30 more years after the first Earth Day—and 50 years after the switch—before the company started even mentioned recycled on its labels, and all the way to 2009 before the company really turned this into a marketing asset.

Not surprisingly, once the company finally started actively bragging, it rapidly became the #1 selling recycled brand in the country, even though its only available in one region of the country.

I have learned not to be shy about listing the benefits of my own offerings. So let me remind you: If you'd like to know more about smart green marketing, pick up a copy of my award-winning and Environmental category bestselling eighth book, Guerrilla Marketing Goes Green: Winning Strategies to Improve Your Profits and Your Planet (co-authored with Jay Conrad Levinson). In addition to getting great advice about how to market green products and services, and how to move toward a greener future, you'll also receive $2000 worth of bonuses if you register your purchase (no matter where you buy it) at <www.guerrillamarketinggoesgreen.com/resources-2/bonuses>.

What Green Marketers Can Learn from Ring Tones

Every mobile phone comes with some ringtones built in. And therefore, nobody actually needs to purchase a ringtone. And yet, at its peak, continuing at least through 2011, the ringtone industry generated more than $4 billion a year (US dollars), worldwide. (The industry is declining, as text supplants voice, and as more phones carry greater options in standard ringer choices.)

$4 billion is a lot of money for something that nobody needs.

Are there lessons in this industry for green marketers? Most certainly. Here are a two among many:

1. We Crave Making Our Mark

The age of individuality goes back at least as far as the Beatnik movement in the 1950s, flowered with the hippies of the 1960s, and continues to spread in our own era. As a society, we each strive to be seen as unique, different.

The conformity of the 1950s gray flannel suit is long gone. Where once there were rules of fashion, now, we have enormous latitude in what we wear. We can mix colors and patterns that would make our parents cringe. Women might wear a miniskirt over a mid-length dress, with leggings underneath. Men have added pink and lavender to their shirt choices.

And perhaps even more than in society as a whole, the green world is populated by people who declare their individuality—not just the off-grid recluse with a two-foot-long beard and a shack made from old car parts, but the suburban housewife who wears upcycled fashion jewelry made from old blue jeans and discarded CDs...the craft brewery customer who seeks out an artisan beer that uses fresh organic grain supplied by a local farmer...the college student who proudly bicycles to class...

We business owners benefit when we celebrate our customers' individuality.

 Toyota had to learn that lesson the hard way. When the Prius was first introduced as a drab sedan with limited color choices, sales were slow. From the car's introduction in 1997 through the end of the original model six years later, only about 123,000 were sold.

When the now-familiar sleek hatchback with its wide variety of color choices was brought to market in 2004, sales jumped dramatically, to 1,192,000 in its 4-year lifespan. In other words, it sold nearly ten times as many, in 2/3 the time. All of a sudden, the car was considered sexy.

The trend continued into the 3rd generation, still in production and including various newer models, including the plug-in, small wagon, and midsize wagon. After four years, Toyota has sold more than 2.3 of them.

2. We will Pay for Practical Value

There is a very practical reason why some people choose to buy a ringtone: they get tired of hearing a ring just like theirs, reaching madly for the phone, and discovering that it was someone else's.

To put this in a green context, I sampled some natural tooth-rinse at a green festival, and liked it enough to buy a container at the show. I've been pleased with the way it makes my mouth feel after daily use, and when I ran out, I bought more. I paid $13.99 for a bottle of fluid that's basically food-grade hydrogen peroxide with peppermint oil. I could probably make my own for two or three dollars, if I could easily locate a source of food-grade peroxide. Or I could go the drug store and buy ordinary peroxide for even less. But it is worth it to me to know that they've tested the formula and got it right, to know they've gone through safety procedures and have packaged it in a way that's convenient to use.

So if you give people reasons based on convenience and practicality, they will buy from you, just as they've bought ringtones.

The Opinions of Others

On a recent trip to New York, we decided to have dinner at our favorite Tibetan restaurant. But we only got as far as the front door.

New York, for several years now, not only grades the sanitation of its tens of thousands of eateries with an A, B, or C, but requires them to post the grade in plain view of the entrance. And this place, where we'd enjoyed several wonderful meals, had been downgraded to a C.

This in a Queens neighborhood that boasts over 100 interesting ethnic restaurants within easy walking distance.

So instead of eating Tibetan, we chose an Indian vegetarian restaurant that we'd also eaten at previously.

The loss of our business is a lesson in third-party validation. If you're in an industry that offers third-party ranking or certification, people will pay attention to how well you rank or whether you do or don't have the certification.

FAIRTRADE
INTERNATIONAL

In the green world, numerous sectors offer certifications that matter. Food businesses can be certified organic, GMO-free, fairly traded, etc.

Buildings and building products can be LEED certified at several different levels.

Green businesses of any type in the US can get certified by Green America, whose silver level is easy to achieve, but whose gold level takes quite a bit of work. (I'm proud to say that my own marketing consulting and copywriting firm was the first business ever to achieve Green America's gold certification, so I speak from direct personal experience.)

 Independent certification is a particularly strong reason to do business together—because a good certification shows that you met independent standards put forth by a theoretically neutral and third party. Note, however, that self-certification will only convince those who can't see through the scheme. You want it come from an outside party.

Certification is a powerful offer of social proof. Social proof is showing that others have made this choice, thus implying that it's a good choice to make. This is why businesses sometimes park employees' vehicles in the customer lot, or run ads with headlines like "98,762 homeowners can't be wrong." (Actually, they could be quite wrong. But that's a discussion for another column.)

In our unvetted society, where the barriers to entry in starting a company, publishing a book, recording a music album, or inventing a new green process have gotten so low that pretty much anyone can do these things, social proof becomes a set of important judging criteria that allow your prospects to sift the offers and choose the ones that are likely to offer quality.

But certification is only one type of social proof among many. You probably already know dozens of ways to get social proof. Here are a few:

- ✓ Reviews in mainstream media

- ✓ Reader reviews on consumer sites

- ✓ Awards

- ✓ Endorsements or testimonials, especially from people who are famous (the most believable identify the actual person's name—not just initials—city, and title/company)

- ✓ Speaking before prestigious organizations

- ✓ Landing a publishing or recording contract with one of the legacy book publishers or recording companies

- ✓ Being interviewed or publishing your own articles in the media

- ✓ Large numbers of engaged followers on social media such as Twitter, LinkedIn, Facebook, and Pinterest

- ✓ Having a Wikipedia page

Actually, my own Wikipedia page is a great example of the power of social proof. Of course, I wanted the page up there to create social proof. But one of the thousands of citizen-editors challenged my page and said it should be taken down because it was too promotional. What got him to back down was when another editor cited the social proof that I've been quoted repeatedly in the New

York Times (widely considered the most authoritative newspaper in the United States and among the top newspapers in the world).

* * *

I enjoyed writing this column from 2010 to 2014, and I think I provided very high value for those who read it. Unfortunately, I never got enough markets to make the project economically viable.

As I move in the direction of helping companies see the value in solving problems like hunger, poverty, war, and climate catastrophe, I can no longer afford the luxury of doing this column for the few markets that subscribed. So this will be the last issue for a while.

I'd love to bring it back, if I can get to a minimum number of subscribers each paying just $10 per month. If you have possible markets for me, please drop me a line at shel AT greenandprofitable.com with the subject "Column Market."

Disclaimer: The very observant among you may notice that some examples come up more than once. Keep in mind that this ebook is a compilation of a monthly column that ran for four years. I have organized the columns by topic rather than chronologically here, and as a result, columns that may have been years apart end up close to each other in the same ebook. Yes, some examples are repeated, but they were inserted to make different points, at different times. Please also note that nothing in this ebook series should be taken as legal or professional advice, and as in any situation, your results may vary as you implement the tips and ideas.

About Shel Horowitz and Business For a Better World

Green business profitability expert Shel Horowitz shows businesses how to profit both by going green and by addressing problems like hunger and poverty, war, violence, and catastrophic climate change. Active in both marketing and the environment since his teen years in the early 1970s, Shel is the award-winning author of eight books including long-running Amazon category bestseller _Guerrilla Marketing Goes Green_.

- ✓ As a consultant, Shel brings laser focus to turning problems into opportunities, opening new markets, and helping you identify potential partners.

- ✓ As a marketing and informational copywriter trained in journalism, Shel is known for his clear writing, ability to make technical concepts accessible, and his skill in telling "the story behind the story" to move people to action.

- ✓ As an international speaker and trainer, Shel combines dynamic vocal style with powerful graphics and gets his audiences actively involved. He's spoken at major business and environmental conferences in locations as diverse as Istanbul, Davos (Switzerland), and Honolulu.

After over a decade actively assisting green businesses with their marketing, Shel branched out in 2014 to help businesses seize profit opportunities in turning hunger and poverty into sufficiency, war and violence into peace, and catastrophic climate change into planetary balance—and helping individuals reclaim their power to actively create this better world.

Shel is happy to talk to you about helping in any of these areas. Reach him at 413-586-2388 (8 a.m. to 10 p.m. US Eastern Time), email shel AT greenandprofitable.com,or find him on Twitter @ShelHorowitz.

Shel also has a gift for you: a free copy of his ebook, *Painless Green: 111 Tips to Help the Environment, Lower Your Carbon Footprint, Cut Your Budget, and Improve Your Quality of Life—With No Negative Impact on Your Lifestyle*. To claim your free copy of this $9.95 ebook, visit PainlessGreenBook.com/earthday and use the code, G&Pebook.

One more set of gifts, FREE with your no-cost subscription to Shel Horowitz's monthly Clean and Green Newsletter:

- ✓ Seven Tips to Gain Marketing Traction as a Green Guerrilla

- ✓ Seven Weeks to a Greener Business: once a week for seven weeks, tips on going greener with printing, energy saving, waste reduction, water conservation, transportation, going deep–green, and of course, green marketing.

- ✓ Plus the informative monthly newsletter, published since 1997 and featuring a business tip or profile plus a book review each issue.

Sign up in the upper-right-hand corner at http://greenandprofitable.com.

www.ingramcontent.com/pod-product-compliance
Lightning Source LLC
Chambersburg PA
CBHW070843180526
45168CB00002B/938